OTHER CAT GIFTBOOKS BY EXLEY:
Cats A Celebration in Words and Paintings
Cat Quotations
The Cat Lover's Address Book
Cat Lover's Notebook

Published simultaneously in 1995 by Exley Publications
in Great Britain, and Exley Giftbooks in the USA.

12 11 10 9 8 7 6 5 4 3 2

Selection and arrangement © Helen Exley 1995.

ISBN 1-85015-629-8

WORDS AND PICTURES SELECTED BY HELEN EXLEY.
RESEARCHED BY MARGARET MONTGOMERY.

Motif artwork by Angela Kerr.
Designed by Pinpoint Design.
Picture research by P.A. Goldberg and J.M. Clift / Image Select, London.
Typeset by Delta, Watford.
Printed at Oriental Press, UAE.

Exley Publications Ltd, 16 Chalk Hill, Watford, Herts WD1 4BN, UK.
Exley Giftbooks, 232 Madison Avenue, Suite 1206, NY 10016, USA.

GLORIOUS
CATS

A COLLECTION OF
WORDS AND PAINTINGS
SELECTED BY
HELEN EXLEY

NEW YORK • WATFORD UK

Cats are the only creatures who know that they are

equal to human beings. Not better than, as the ancient

Egyptians thought, and not less than, as most of us

continue to believe. Just equal. It's knowledge that

all kittens are born with, and however much

we vacillate between one socio-philosophical theory

and another, cats – who formed their opinions

about most things several million years ago –

see no reason for blowing their minds

with questions about equality at this late date.

JUDY GARDINER, FROM "*CAT CHAT*"

I love cats. I love their grace and their elegance. I love their independence and their arrogance, and the way they lie and look at you, summing you up, surely to your detriment, with that unnerving, unwinking, appraising stare.

JOYCE STRANGER, FROM "KYM"

Her ears, lightly fringed with white that looked silver, lifted and moved, back, forward, listening and sensing. Her face turned, slightly, after each new sensation, alert. Her tail moved, in another dimension, as if its tip was catching messages her other organs could not. She sat poised, air-light, looking, hearing, feeling, smelling, breathing, with all of her, fur, whiskers, ears – everything, in delicate vibration. If a fish is the movement of water embodied, given shape, then cat is a diagram and pattern of subtle air.

DORIS LESSING, FROM
"*PARTICULARLY CATS AND MORE CATS*"

His advances were subtle: a movement of his head, a light grazing of our legs with his flank, a glance, a moment of purring. Unobvious things that we gradually learned to observe and interpret. The nearest Rabbit came to effusiveness was rolling – his speciality. He would sink down in a long, slow glide until his head touched the floor, then deftly throw himself over on his back, wiggling his hind paws in a supreme gesture of good will. But a cat usually writes his love notes in shorthand and reading them demands a certain amount of practice.

LLOYD ALEXANDER

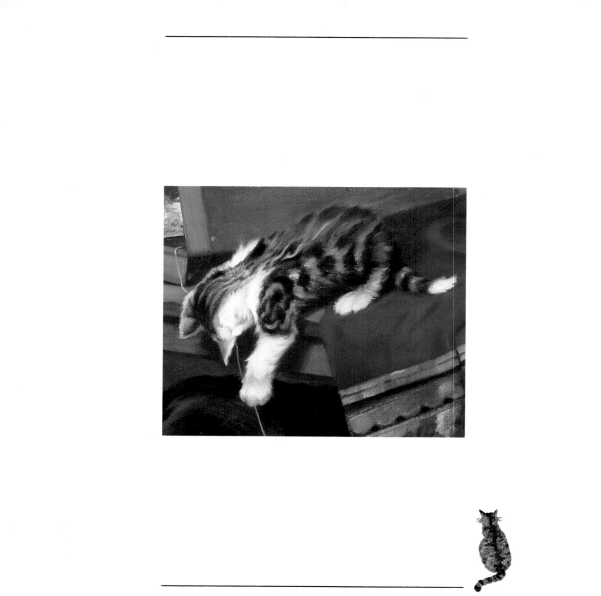

The playful kitten,
with its pretty little tigerish gambols,
is infinitely more amusing than half
the people one is obliged to live with
in the world.

LADY SYDNEY MORGAN

The fact is that, to cats, we humans
are, for all our grotesque size,
unbelievably slow and clumsy.
We are totally incapable
of managing a good leap or jump
or pounce or swipe.

CLEVELAND AMORY

When I play with my cat
who knows whether I do not make her more sport
than she makes me?

MICHEL DE MONTAIGNE

But under the fur,
whatever colour it may be,
there still lies,
essentially unchanged,
one of the world's free souls.

ERIC GURNEY, FROM

"HOW TO LIVE WITH A CALCULATING CAT."

Her prettiest trick, used mostly for company, was to lie on her back under a sofa and pull herself along by her paws, in fast sharp rushes, stopping to turn her elegant little head sideways, yellow eyes narrowed, waiting for applause. "Oh beautiful kitten! Delicious beast! Pretty cat!" Then on she went for another display.

Or, on the right surface, the yellow carpet, a blue cushion, she lay on her back and slowly rolled, paws tucked up, head back, so that her creamy chest and stomach were exposed, marked faintly, as if she were a delicate subspecies of leopard, with black blotches, like the roses

of leopards. *"Oh beautiful kitten, oh you
are so beautiful."* And she was prepared to
go on until the compliments stopped.

DORIS LESSING, FROM
"PARTICULARLY CATS AND MORE CATS"

*H*ow many times have I rested tired eyes on her graceful little body, curled up in a ball and wrapped round with her tail like a parcel; or stretched out luxuriously on my bed, one paw covering her face, the other curved gently inwards, as though clasping an invisible treasure. Asleep or awake, in rest, in motion, grave or gay, Agrippina is always beautiful; and it is better to be beautiful than to fetch and carry from the rising to the setting of the sun.

Oh, you who strive to relieve your overwrought nerves, cultivate power through repose, watch the exquisite languor of a drowsy cat and despair of imitating such perfect and restful grace. There is a gradual yielding of every muscle to the soft persuasiveness of slumber; the flexible frame is curved into tender lines, the head nestles lower, the paws are tucked out of sight; no convulsive throb or start betrays a rebellious alertness; only a faint quiver of unconscious satisfaction, a faint heaving of the tawny sides, a faint gleam of the half-shut eyes, and Agrippina is asleep. I look at her for one wistful moment and then turn resolutely to my work. It were ignoble to wish myself in her place; and yet how charming to be able to settle down to a nap *sans peur et sans reproche* at ten o'clock in the morning.

AGNES REPPLIER

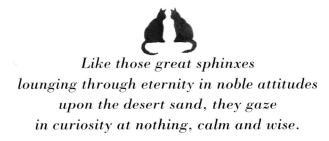

Like those great sphinxes
lounging through eternity in noble attitudes
upon the desert sand, they gaze
in curiosity at nothing, calm and wise.

CHARLES BAUDELAIRE

Cats do not merely demand civilization.
They create it.

T. O. BEACHCROFT

I've met many thinkers and many cats,
but the wisdom of cats is infinitely superior.

HIPPOLYTE TAINE

ATOSSA
Cruel, but composed and bland,
Dumb, inscrutable and grand,
So Tiberius might have sat
Had Tiberius been a cat.

MATTHEW ARNOLD

He [the cat] is entirely self-reliant. He lives in homes because he chooses to do so, and as long as the surroundings and the people suit him; but he lives there on his own terms, and never sacrifices his own comfort or his own well-being for the sake of the stupid folk with whom he comes in contact. Thus he is the most satisfactory of friends....

The cat neither gives nor accepts invitations that do not come from the heart.... If he wishes to move, he does so: perhaps to the wilds, perhaps to another house.

CARL VAN VECHTEN, FROM *"THE TIGER IN THE HOUSE"*

For most of us an open book means a cat on top of it. To sit in a comfortable chair means getting there a split second before a cat – and having to suffer its resentful stares as a consequence. It may infiltrate behind you – and shove. Or sit on the arm – and lean. Or wrap itself round your neck – and throttle. Or touch you lightly with persuasive paw or gentle nose ... until, of course, you give in.

Two cats mean one on the knee and one trying to get it off by licks, kisses, pokes, snarls or simply sitting on top of it. Or the second one will lie on your chest, suspended over the first like an imminent avalanche, of which the first is fully aware.

More than two cats means eyes. All accusing you of favouritism and deep unkindness.

PAM BROWN

*T*hough the cats drove visitors nearly mad with their attentions when they first arrived, however, if anybody stayed after eleven o'clock things were very different. Then, retiring to the most comfortable arm-chair (if anybody was sitting in it they just squeezed down behind him and kept turning round and round till he got out; it never failed), they curled up and ostentatiously tried to go to sleep. Tried was the operative word. Any time anybody looked across at the chair there would be at least one Siamese regarding them with half-raised head, one eye open and a pained expression that clearly indicated it was time they went home. Some People were tired. If this had no effect, in due course Solomon would sit up, yawn noisily, and subside again with a loud sigh on top of Sheba. Few visitors missed that hint. Solomon yawned like fat men belch – long, loudly and with gusto. What was most embarrassing, though, was the way – after lying for hours as if they'd been working all day in a chain gang – they suddenly perked up the moment people did start to go. It wouldn't have been so bad if they'd just politely seen them off at the door, the way Sugieh used to do. These two sat in the hall and bawled to people to hurry up – and as we shepherded people to the front gate they could be seen quite plainly through the window, hilariously chasing one another over the chairs by way of celebration.

DOREEN TOVEY, FROM *"CATS IN THE BELFRY"*

THE CAT AND THE MOON

The cat went here and there
And the moon spun round like a top,
And the nearest kin of the moon,
The creeping cat, looked up.
Black Minnaloushe stared at the moon,
For, wander and wail as he would,
The pure cold light in the sky
Troubled his animal blood.
Minnaloushe runs in the grass
Lifting his delicate feet.

Do you dance, Minnaloushe, do you dance?
When two close kindred meet,
What better than call a dance?
Maybe the moon may learn,
Tired of that courtly fashion,
A new dance turn.
Minnaloushe creeps through the grass
From moonlit place to place,
The sacred moon overhead
Has taken a new phase.
Does Minnaloushe know that his pupils
Will pass from change to change,
And that from round to crescent,
From crescent to round they range?
Minnaloushe creeps through the grass
Alone, important and wise,
And lifts to the changing moon
His changing eyes.

W. B. YEATS

That cat [Samantha] is in love with me, but to say that it's "mutual" doesn't begin to describe anything. I'm totally irrational about her. She and I are a scandal.

HELEN GURLEY BROWN

Slowly, with a look of intense concentration, he got up and advanced on me, like Tarquin with ravishing strides, poised himself, put out a front paw, and stroked my cheek as I used to stroke his chops. A human caress from a cat. I felt very meagre and ill-educated that I could not purr.

SYLVIA TOWNSEND WARNER

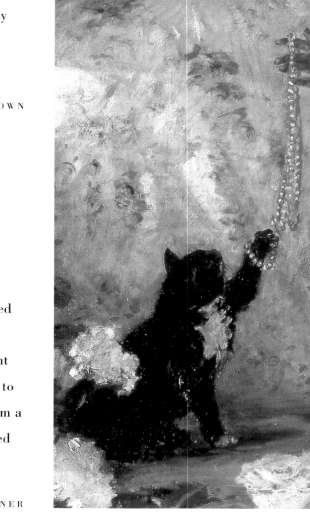

... there is always the lurking suspicion in all of us of the power of the cupboard. Was there in bygone days a real cat deity, a supercat who one moment, smitten with a stroke of genius, discovered and imparted to all that followed it that man is the eternal sucker who can be flattered or conned into anything with the right approach? When oft-times we are compelled to the same doubts as to the sincerity of the fervent declarations of undying passion from members of our own kind, what is so strange in suspecting that our cat maybe is putting on the act of the ages? In fact, one would have to be wholly besotted with one's own worth <u>not</u> to wonder, knowing the cat's reserve and independence. Suspicion is further an outgrowth of the fact that they can turn it on and they can turn it off. And if, for the most part you seem to remember that they turn it on when there would appear to be something in it for them, then you suddenly remember that day when you sat depressed in a chair, suffering from a hurt concealed, a worry, a disappointment, or a crisis, and suddenly there was someone soft and furry in your lap and a body pressed close to yours in warmth and comfort.

PAUL GALLICO, FROM *"HONOURABLE CAT"*

… kittens share to a high degree those qualities of charm, helplessness, and appeal which are common to the very young – even to the human baby. The mere word "kitten" immediately conjures up a small furry fubsy warm and engaging creature with eyes hardly open, paws too big for its body, a squeak of a voice, and an insatiable appetite. This picture is followed almost immediately by a second one of several kittens together; jumping at flies or leaves or shadows; chasing each other or their own tails; growling in mimic combat; curled up together in a basket, sleeping with expressions improbably angelic. A kitten can imitate the original Unrepentant Thief and never fail to find excuse.

VAL GIELGUD,
FROM *"CATS. A PERSONAL ANTHOLOGY"*

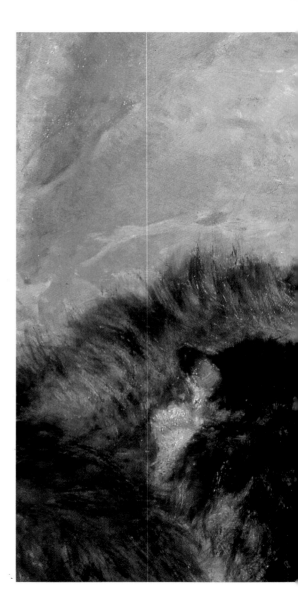

Kittens, kittens, showers of kittens, visitations of kittens. So many, you see them as Kitten, like leaves growing on a bare branch, staying heavy and green, then falling, exactly the same every year. People coming to visit say: What happened to that lovely kitten? What lovely kitten? They are all lovely kittens.

Kitten. A tiny lively creature in its transparent membrane, surrounded by the muck of its birth. Ten minutes later, damp but clean, already at the nipple. Ten days later, a minute scrap with soft hazy eyes, its mouth opening in a hiss of brave defiance at the enormous menace sensed bending over it. At this point, in the wild, it would confirm wildness, become wild cat. But no, a human hand touches it, the human smell envelops it, a human voice reassures it. Soon it gets out of its nest, confident that the gigantic creatures all around will do it no harm. It totters, then strolls, then runs all over the house. It squats in its earth box, licks itself, sips milk, then tackles a rabbit bone, defends it against the rest of the litter. Enchanting kitten, pretty kitten, beautiful furry babyish delicious little beast — then off it goes.

DORIS LESSING, FROM *"PARTICULARLY CATS AND MORE CATS"*

In the presence of strangers [your cat] is capable of ignoring you completely. "What a beautiful cat," exclaims your guest. If you are unwise in the ways of cats, you will commit the indiscretion of calling the cat to you. There is an awkward pause, while your cat reflectively examines a dainty paw, or a table leg. Foolishly, you call again. Your cat looks in the opposite direction, yawns gracefully and strolls off with an air of complete unconcern.

Worse still, your cat will sometimes display a perverse affection for your visitors. This usually happens on top of your boasting about the wretched animal's peculiar devotion to yourself. To make matters worse, the object of his temporary affections is, as like as not, someone who is not interested in cats or even actively dislikes them. How often have I heard people say, "Isn't it strange? I don't like cats but they always come to me." And the explanation? I suspect cats, and my own in particular, of a wayward and discreditable sense of humour.

MICHAEL JOSEPH. FROM *"CAT'S COMPANY"*

Cats may not be our servants
or our defenders,
but give us life.
Lying softly in laps, tuning their
*   heartbeats to our own,*
singing away sorrow,
easing the mind,
unravelling the day.
Sharing the empty dark.
Like flowers, inexhaustible in beauty.
Like flowers, most necessary –
in ways we scarcely understand.
Healers, Companions.
Mysteries.

PAM BROWN

Among human beings
a cat is merely a cat;
among cats a cat is
a prowling shadow
in a jungle.

KAREL ČAPEK

House Cat jumping, pouncing, playing, rolling, cruising; each of these has its moments of supreme delectation. Nothing the animal does is ungraceful.

But I think a cat at rest with me in the same room is what I like best. The curl-up in a perfect circle or sometimes with one paw over its eyes as though to shut out the light; the hunker with all four feet tidily tucked under, or the sit-up with its tail neatly tucked around its bottom. The poses I know are sheer vanity, for cats are indeed vain and like to be admired. But they will choose backgrounds and put themselves into positions which they know are admirable. They will drape their bodies to the shape of a piece of furniture. They will hang a paw in what seems to be a wholly casual manner, but you know and they know damn well that it is studied. But it is never wrong. Merely by the turn of their heads upon their necks, a half an inch or so, they can change the picture and give expression to some inner feeling and, by doing so, set up a glow of appreciation in the watcher.

Well, and as for words, they define less than House Cat illustrates them: aesthetic, sublime, tragic, comic; symmetry, supremacy, dignity, charm and grace; in short, the beautiful.

PAUL GALLICO, FROM *"HONOURABLE CAT"*

Who can believe that there is no soul behind those luminous eyes!

THÉOPHILE GAUTIER

In grey cat's eyes lay the green sheen of a jade butterfly's wing, as if an artist had said: what could be as graceful, as delicate as a cat? What more naturally the creature of the air? What air-being has affinity with cat? Butterfly, butterfly of course! And there, deep in cat's eyes lies this thought, hinted at merely, with a half-laugh; and hidden behind the fringes of lashes, behind the fine brown inner lid, and the evasions of cat-coquetry.

Grey cat, perfect, exquisite, a queen; grey cat with her hints of leopard and snake; suggestions of butterfly and owl; a miniature lion steel-clawed for murder, grey cat full of secrets, affinities, mysteries....

DORIS LESSING,
"PARTICULARLY CATS AND MORE CATS"

For the study of majestic dignity, tinged on occasions with lofty disdain, interpreters of muscular expression would do well to seek out Adolphus. He walks the highway without haste or concern for his personal survival in the midst of tooting automobiles and charging dogs. When a strange dog appears and mistakes Adolphus for an ordinary cat who may be chased for the sport of the thing, it is the custom of Adolphus to slow his pace somewhat and stretch out in the path of the oncoming enemy, assuming the pose and the expression of the sphinx. He is the graven image of repose and perfect muscular control. Only his slumbrous amber eyes burn unblinkingly, never leaving the enraged countenance of his enemy, who bears down upon him with exposed fangs and hackles erect. When the assault is too ferocious to be in good taste even among dogs, accompanied by hysterical yapping and snapping, Adolphus has been known to yawn in the face of his assailant, quite deliberately and very politely, as a gentleman of good breeding might when bored by an excessive display of emotion. Usually the dog mysteriously halts within a foot or so of those calm yellow eyes and describes a semi-circle within the range of those twin fires, filling the air with defiant taunts that gradually die away to foolish whimpering as he begins an undignified withdrawal, while Adolphus winks solemnly and stares past his cowering foe into a mysterious space undesecrated by blustering dogs.

N. MARGARET CAMPBELL

...most people who condemn the cat for his apparent lack of devotion do so without giving a thought to what is required of them before they can qualify for it. A cat does not ask to be petted and treated indulgently. Indeed, to patronize a cat with superficial endearments is more likely to offend than gratify him. A cat wants, first of all, to be understood. How can a cat respect a human being so senseless and inconsiderate as not to know when a door or window must be opened? Or when he wants to be intelligently admired or talked to?

MICHAEL JOSEPH, FROM *"CAT'S COMPANY"*

Those who love cats which do not even purr,
Or which are thin and tired and very old,
Bend down to them in the street and stroke their fur
And rub their ears and smooth their breast, and hold
Their paws, and gaze into their eyes of gold.

FRANCIS SCARFE

... we have kinship with the cats. They are unhappy in the presence of dirt, bad smells, and corruption. Is it perhaps that we can see ourselves, condemned by misfortune to such a life where for sustenance we might have to nose through garbage pails and offal disposal? One is never so high that one cannot be brought low, and the stray produces for us a picture of the depths.

PAUL GALLICO, FROM "*HONOURABLE CAT*"

... nearly all will agree that the best purr of all, the purr that speaks most directly to the heart, is the first faint purr that comes from a frightened stray, that one has found in the rain and taken in one's arms and coaxed with confidence. This is the purr that is quite irresistible, the language that only a brute would fail to heed.

BEVERLEY NICHOLS, FROM "*CATS' A-Z*"

Our cats might not be wizards of the Stock Market but there was little doubt that they would have made wonderful actors....

As a combination they were irresistible, and well they knew it. Nobody would think, when we had visitors and they sat side by side on the hearth-rug with Sheba demurely reaching up to wash Solomon's ears and Solomon occasionally retaliating with an affectionate slurp that nearly knocked her off her feet, that right before the doorbell rang they had been fighting like a couple of alley cats over who was going to have first place on Charles's lap. Nobody would think – seeing them trotting meekly down the hill behind the Rector, who had for the umpteenth time that week found them sitting outside his front gate wailing that they were lost – that to their dear little minds it was the side-splitting equivalent of ringing doorbells and running away. Nobody except us, who had seen them marching determinedly up the hill in the first place, ignoring our appeals to come back and changing their pace to a forlorn meander before our very eyes as they rounded the corner.

And even we were flabbergasted when we heard that when we were at the office they could be seen in the hall window every afternoon at four-thirty, gazing wistfully up the hill and imploring passers-by to tell them when we were coming home. When we got in just after five they were always Sound Asleep in an arm-chair and there was such an exhibition of opening one eye, yawning and complete astonishment that we were back so soon that we could hardly believe it.

DOREEN TOVEY, FROM *"CATS IN THE BELFRY"*

*W*hen I was making the bed, she was happy to be made into it; and stayed, visible as a tiny lump, quite happily, sometimes for hours, between the blankets. If you stroked the lump, it purred and mewed. But she would not come out until she had to.

The lump would move across the bed, hesitate at the edge. There might be a frantic mew as she slid to the floor. Dignity disturbed, she licked herself hastily, glaring yellow eyes at the viewers, who made a mistake if they laughed. Then, every hair conscious of itself, she walked to some centre stage….

She was as arrogantly aware of herself as a pretty girl who has no attributes but her prettiness….

Cat, at the age when, if she were human, she would be wearing clothes and hair like weapons, but confident that any time she chose she might relapse into indulged childhood again, because the role had become too much of a burden – cat posed and princessed and preened about the house and then, tired, a little peevish, tucked herself into the fold of a newspaper or behind a cushion, and watched the world safely from there.

DORIS LESSING. FROM "*PARTICULARLY CATS AND MORE CATS*"

*H*e is modest. He is urbane. He is dignified. Indeed a well-bred cat never argues. He goes about doing what he likes in a well-bred superior manner. If he is interrupted he will look at you in mild surprise or silent reproach, but he will return to his desire. If he is prevented, he will wait for a more favourable occasion. But like all well-bred individualists, and unlike human anarchists, the cat seldom interferes with other people's rights. His intelligence keeps him from doing many of the fool things that complicate life. Cats never write operas, and they never attend them. They never sign papers, or pay taxes, or vote for presidents. An injunction will have no power whatever over a cat. A cat, of course, would not only refuse to obey any amendment whatever to any constitution. He would refuse to obey the Constitution itself.

CARL VAN VECHTEN, FROM *"THE TIGER IN THE HOUSE"*

A blazing fire, a warm rug, candles lit and curtains drawn, the kettle on for tea, and finally the cat before you, attracting your attention – it is a scene which everybody likes. The cat purrs, as if it applauded our consideration, and gently moves its tail.... Now she proceeds to clean herself all over ... beginning with her paws, and fetching amazing tongues at her hind-hips. Anon, she scratches her neck with a foot of rapid delight, leaning her head towards it, and shutting her eyes half to accommodate the action of the skin and half to enjoy the luxury. She then rewards her paws with a few more touches – look at the action of her head and neck, how pleasing it is, the ears pointed forward, and the neck gently arching to and fro. Finally she gives a sneeze, and another twist of mouth and whiskers, and then, curling her tail towards her front claws settles herself on her hind quarters in an attitude of bland meditation....

LEIGH HUNT

Oh cat; I'd say, or pray: be-ooootiful cat! Delicious cat! Exquisite cat! Satiny cat! Cat like a soft owl, cat with paws like moths, jewelled cat, miraculous cat! Cat, cat, cat, cat.

She would ignore me first; then turn her head, silkily arrogant, and half close her eyes for each praise-name, each one separately. And, when I'd finished, yawn, deliberate, foppish, showing an ice-cream-pink mouth and curled pink tongue.

DORIS LESSING, FROM *"PARTICULARLY CATS AND MORE CATS"*

The smallest feline is a

masterpiece LEONARDO DA VINCI

*With his tail, with his paws, his cocking ears, his eyes, his
head, the turn of his body, or the waving of his fur, he
expresses in symbols the most cabalistic secrets. He is
beautiful, and he is graceful. He makes his appearance and
his life as exquisite as circumstances will permit.*

CARL VAN VECHTEN, FROM *"THE TIGER IN THE HOUSE"*

"Amathea, most beautiful of cats, why have you deigned to single me out for so much favour? Did you recognize in me a friend to all that breathes? Or were you yourself suffering from loneliness (though I take it you are near your own dear home)? Or is there pity in the hearts of animals as there is in the hearts of some humans? What then was your motive? Or am I, indeed, foolish to ask, and not rather to take whatever good comes to me in whatever way from the gods?"

To these questions Amathea answered with a loud purring noise, expressing with closed eyes of ecstasy her delight in the encounter.

"I am more than flattered, Amathea," said I by way of answer; "I am consoled. I did not know that there was in the world anything breathing and moving, let alone one so tawny-perfect, who would give companionship for its own sake and seek out, through deep feeling, some one companion out of all living kind…."

To this Amathea made a slight gesture of acknowledgment – not disdainful – wagging her head a little, and then settling it down in deep content.

"Oh, beautiful-haired Amathea, many have praised you before you found me to praise you; and many will praise you, some in your own tongue, when I am no longer held in the bonds of your presence. But none will praise you more sincerely. For there is not a man living who knows better than I that the four charms of a cat lie in its closed eyes, its long and lovely hair, its silence, and even its affected love."

HILAIRE BELLOC,   FROM *"CONVERSATION WITH A CAT"*

The comfort of "One" and "Four" was a first priority as soon as we arrived at Merry Hall, and I shall never forget the afternoon when I took them for their first really "country" walk round the huge, deserted old garden. It was an experience so enchanting that it was almost worth buying the house, even for that. The first pause on the steps, with one front paw lifted up in a sort of curve of interrogation … the blinking around at the vast prospect before them … the venturing forth … the suspicious pause before the long grass … the glancing around over their shoulders at me, their master, to inquire if it was politic to enter this jungle … and then, the sudden dive into the grass, and the tails waving – … and the weavings and the scurryings and the tumblings and the chasings, and the sudden plaintive wails from "Four" when he felt lost, and had to be lifted up, and have the grass seeds wiped from the corners of his eyes.

And then – the first dash up the trunk of the first apple tree in the orchard, and the quivering progress along the branches, with crossed feet and twitching tails, and the green eyes staring up in amazement at this strange leafy paradise.

BEVERLEY NICHOLS, FROM *"THE GIFT OF A HOME"*

As a companion puss is not without blemish. No one so thoroughly selfish as the cat can supply perfect companionship. For him the time, the place and the loved one have to be harmonized, and then, if he feels like it, he may condescend to honour you with his company. Yet the cat's attitude is clearly consistent. He does what pleases him. You may be sure when a cat sits purring contentedly on your knee that he is not doing it to please you. Realize this – and sooner or later all familiar with cats do realize it – and thus administer a salutary check to the vanity fostered in all of us by animal companions.

MICHAEL JOSEPH, FROM "CAT'S COMPANY"

The cat's place in the home is something rather more than a mere ornamentation of the hearth. It is an essential part of the background to a man's refuge; and without it one could say that no home is ever quite complete.

A cat may – and often does – spend as much time outside the home as within it, but his attachment to its interior, like our own, is none the less....

For ourselves <u>his</u> presence is of no less importance. His miaou of welcome upon our return, whether he is waiting for us on the doorstep, or whether he is inside, perched upon the arm of a chair, is a gentle pleasurable sound ... the touch of his head as he rubs it affectionately against our legs, gives us a sense of calm after the busy crowds who have jostled us; and there, within the walls which detach us from some of the cares that have infested the day, we realize that his presence seems, somehow, to symbolize our Place of Peace.

FRANK CREW, FROM "DEVOTED TO CATS"

He was a cat of acute perceptions.
He knew at once
when I was melancholy or depressed,
and had his own ways
of comforting me.
If I were in a bad temper
he was silent and unobtrusive,
waiting for my evil mood to pass.
When I was cheerful
and ready for play, so was he.
There were days when I had to stay in bed,
and then he rarely left me.
Not even the glowing sun outside
could lure him from my room.
His devotion
when he knew that something was amiss
with me moved me deeply.

MICHAEL JOSEPH, FROM
"CHARLES: THE STORY OF A FRIENDSHIP"

Sugieh fell in love with us the moment she saw us. It was most embarrassing because we had made up our minds to have a Seal Point like Mimi, and when the breeder said all the Seal Point kittens had gone but perhaps we would like to see the two Blue Points that were left it was understood that we did so merely out of interest. Unfortunately nobody had told Sugieh that … Sugieh … was quite certain we had come for her. She sat there on the hearthrug like a small girl with her suitcase packed ready to go on holiday – her eyes screwed tight with anticipation, her paws pounding up and down like little pistons. When I got down on my knees and spoke to her she opened her eyes for a moment – … completely crossed with excitement – greeted us with a squawk that was astounding, considering her size, and screwed them up tight again, waiting for the treat….

… When we left she went with us….

DOREEN TOVEY, FROM *"CATS IN THE BELFRY"*

" C A T "

Tearaway kitten or staid mother of fifty,
Persian, Chinchilla, Siamese
Or backstreet brawler – you all have a tiger in your blood
And eyes opaque as the sacred mysteries.

The hunter's instinct sends you pouncing, dallying,
Formal and wild as a temple dance.
You take from man what is your due – the fireside saucer,
And give him his – a purr of tolerance.

Like poets you wrap your solitude around you
And catch your meaning unawares:
With consequential trot or frantic tarantella
You follow up your top-secret affairs.

Simpkin, our pretty cat, assumes my lap
As a princess her rightful throne,
Pads round and drops asleep there. Each is a familiar
Warmth to the other, each no less alone.

CECIL DAY LEWIS,   FROM "THE BEST CAT STORIES"

ON A NIGHT OF SNOW

Cat, if you go outdoors you must walk in the snow,
You will come back with little white shoes on your feet,
Little white slippers of snow that have heels of sleet.
Stay by the fire, my Cat. Lie still, do not go.
See how the flames are leaping and hissing low,
I will bring you a saucer of milk like a marguerite,
So white and so smooth, so spherical and so sweet –
Stay with me, Cat. Outdoors the wild winds blow.

Outdoors the wild winds blow, Mistress, and dark is the night.
Strange voices cry in the trees, intoning strange lore,
And more than cats move, lit by our eyes' green light,
On silent feet where the meadow grasses hang hoar –
Mistress, there are portents abroad of magic and might,
And things that are yet to be done. Open the door.

ELIZABETH J. COATSWORTH

Sass … can jump like a Mexican bean. When we take them over to the orchard he soars spectacularly over the bars which block the entrance – up, over and down from standing, to the astonishment of all who see him, while Shebalu clambers primly over them like one of the "Pirates of Penzance" girls over the rocks. Indoors, however, it is she who leaps without a second thought five feet up to the back window of the living-room – the high one that looks out on to the hillside where Annabel and her friends the magpies roam. And what does Sass the Indomitable do when, seeing her craning her neck at something that appears to be interesting, he decides to join her in the window sill? He clambers laboriously, as he did when a kitten, up the back of one of our antique carved chairs.

Then it was delightful, watching him heave his small white body up the pattern of acorns and dog-roses like a climber ascending the Matterhorn, invariably losing his nerve halfway up and bawling for a leg-up over the top. But when the tallest cat we have ever had, who, standing on his hind legs, now reaches a good three-quarters of the way up the chair-back before he even starts, <u>still</u> clambers babyishly up the carving, <u>still</u> bawls for help because he's stuck and has, into the bargain, left a permanent trail of scratches over the acorns to mark his passage....

What, I sometimes ask, will they think of to ruin next? Why do they always pick on something that might one day, if they hadn't mucked it up, have been valuable? Why on earth, with all the experience we've had, do we go on having … cats? Then I see Sass … looking at me out of that anxious, pointed face – and I pick him up and hug him. That is my answer.

DOREEN TOVEY, FROM *"A COMFORT OF CATS"*

IT FILLED MY HEART WITH LOVE

When I hold in my hand a soft and crushable animal,

and feel the fur beat for fear and the soft feather, I cannot

feel unhappy.

In his fur the animal rode, and in his fur he strove,

And oh it filled my heart my heart, it filled my heart

with love.

STEVIE SMITH

I adore cats. I do not mind them at all when they scrape their exquisite claws all down one's best armchair. I have not the heart to reprimand them when they push a cold, purring nose against an ornament and whisk it off my desk … because their expression of faint disdain as they regard the ornament, after it has been foolish enough to fall to the floor, is worth any ornament that was ever made.

BEVERLEY NICHOLS, FROM *"DOWN THE GARDEN PATH"*

It is strange that it has taken so long for the medical profession to realize that a small animal can ease stress and pain and loneliness in the old and the ill.

A cat or dog does not help merely by being soft and warm and alive, but by telling the human being that it does not matter if she or he is old or ugly, helpless or confused. It does not matter that they have failed, if they are poor, or that the world seems to have no further use for them. An animal sees the self that has never changed since it was new born, the young soul that occupies the old or injured body. The kind young nurses smile – but they do not know the person in their care is the same age as themselves, trapped in a body they barely recognize as their own. An animal makes no such mistake.

They are like us. A young cat looks out of a body grown gaunt with age. We share this strange phenomenon of eternal youth. We all die young.

I lack all certainty
yet still I hope
that at the edge of death I'll see
a small cat racing from the dark
to welcome me.

PAM BROWN

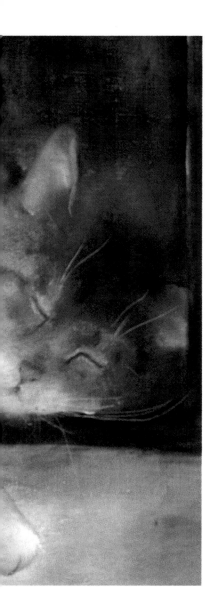

ON A CAT AGEING

He blinks upon the hearth-rug
And yawns in deep content
Accepting all the comforts
That Providence has sent.

Louder he purrs, and louder,
In one glad hymn of praise
For all the night's adventures,
For quiet restful days.

Life will go on for ever,
With all that cat can wish:
Warmth, and the glad procession
Of fish, and milk and fish.

Only – the thought disturbs him –
He's noticed once or twice,
The times are somehow breeding
A nimbler race of mice.

ALEXANDER GRAY

ACKNOWLEDGEMENTS: The Publishers are grateful for permission to reproduce copyright material. Every effort has been made to trace copyright holders, but the publishers would be pleased to hear from any not here acknowledged. HILAIRE BELLOC: extract from "Conversation with a Cat" published by Duckworth, reprinted by permission of Peters, Fraser and Dunlop Group Ltd.; N. MARGARET CAMPBELL: extract from "Best Cat Stories"; ELIZABETH COATSWORTH: "On a Night of Snow" published by Crovell, Collier and Macmillan Inc; FRANK CREW: extract from "Devoted to Cats" published by Frederick Muller Ltd.; PAUL GALLICO: Extracts from "Honourable Cat" © 1972 Paul Gallico and Mathemata Anstalt, reprinted by permission of Souvenir Press and Crown Publishers, Inc., and Aitken, Stone and Wylie Ltd.; JUDY GARDINER: extract from "Cat Chat" published by Frederick Muller, 1978; VAL GIELGUD: extract from "Cats A Personal Anthology", published by Newnes, 1966; MICHAEL JOSEPH: extracts from "Cat's Company" published by Michael Joseph, 1946 and from "Charles: The Story of a Friendship" published by Michael Joseph, 1943; DORIS LESSING: extracts from "Particularly Cats and More Cats" published by Michael Joseph, 1989, © Doris Lessing Productions Ltd. 1967, 1989, reprinted by permission of Michael Joseph Ltd.and Jonathan Clowes Ltd., London, on behalf of Doris Lessing; CECIL DAY LEWIS: "Cat" from "The Best Cat Stories", published by Sinclair Stevenson Ltd., 1969; BEVERLEY NICHOLS: extracts from "Cats' A-Z" © 1977 Beverley Nichols; from "The Gift of a Home" published by W.H.Allen 1972; and from "Down the Garden Path", © Jonathan Cape, 1932, reprinted by permission of Eric Glass Ltd. on behalf of The Estate Of Beverley Nichols; AGNES REPPLIER: extract from "Cat's Company" by Michael Joseph published by Michael Joseph, 1946 reprinted by permission of Penguin Books Ltd.; FRANCES SCARFE: extract from "Old Cats"; STEVIE SMITH: "It Filled My Heart With Love" from "Collected Poems" ed. James MacGibbon, published by Penguin Books Ltd.; DOREEN TOVEY: extracts from "Cats in the Belfry" published by Bantam, 1993 a division of Transworld Publishers Ltd.; extract from "A Comfort of Cats" published by Michael Joseph, 1979, reprinted by permission of Penguin Books Ltd.; CARL VAN VECHTEN: extracts from "The Tiger in the House" © 1920, 1936 Carl van Vechten, reprinted by permission of Alfred Knopf Inc.; W. B. YEATS: "The Cat and the Moon" taken from "Collected Poems", Macmillan.

PICTURE CREDITS:

Exley Publications is very grateful to the following individuals and organisations for permission to reproduce their pictures. Whilst all reasonable efforts have been made to clear copyright and acknowledge sources and artists, Exley Publications would be happy to hear from any copyright holder who may have been omitted.

Front Cover: **"On le Laisse Dormir"** © 1995 Dede Moser.

Title Page: **"Mother's Love"**, Henriette Ronner-Knip (1821-1909), Gavin Graham Gallery, London, Fine Art Photographic Library.

Page 7: **"Troublesome Twins"**, Henriette Ronner-Knip (1821-1909), Fine Art Photographic Library.

Page 8/9: **"Winter Prospect With Cats"** © 1995 Timothy Easton, The Bridgeman Art Library.

Page 10/11: **"Le Chat Tigre"**, Charles van den Eycken (1859-1923), Edimedia.

Page 12: **"Cat Lying Near Fireplace"**, Images Colour Library.

Page 14: **"A Teasing Twosome"** © 1995 Wright Barker (1864-1941), Fine Art Photographic Library.

Page 16/17: **"Le Chat dans le Neige"**, © 1995 Bruno Liljefors (1860-1939), Edimedia.

Page 19: **"Le Studio de L'Artiste"**, Charles van den Eycken (1859-1923), Edimedia.

Page 21: **"A Cosy Spot"**, H. A. Beer, Gavin Graham Gallery, Fine Art Photographic Gallery.

Page 23: **"Katzen"** © 1995 Theophile Alexandre Steinlen, Musee du Petit Palais, Genf, Archiv Fur Kunst, Berlin.

Page 25: **"Le Chat à la Fenetre"**, Hiroshigo (1857), Galerie Janette, Paris, Giraudon.

Page 26/27: **"On le Laisse Dormir"** © 1995 Dede Moser.